CELEBRATION SERIES®

THE PIANO ODYSSEY®

PIANO
REPERTOIRE

10

ISBN 0-88797-703-0

FREDERICK
HARRIS
MUSIC

CELEBRATION SERIES®
THE PIANO ODYSSEY®

The *Celebration Series®* was originally published in 1987 to international acclaim. In 1994, a second edition was released and received with heightened enthusiasm. Launched in 2001 and building on the success of previous editions, the *Celebration Series®, The Piano Odyssey®* takes advantage of the wealth of new repertoire and the changing interests and needs of teachers.

The series is breathtaking in its scope, presenting a true musical odyssey through the ages and their respective musical styles. The albums are graded from late elementary to early intermediate (albums Introductory to 3) through intermediate (albums 4 to 8) to advanced and concert repertoire (albums 9 and 10). Each volume of repertoire comprises a carefully selected grouping of pieces from the Baroque, Classical, Romantic, and 20th-century style periods. *Studies/Etudes* albums present compositions especially suited for building technique as well as musicality relevant to the repertoire of each level. *Student Workbooks* and recordings are available to assist in the study and enjoyment of the music. In addition, the comprehensive *Handbook for Teachers* is an invaluable pedagogical resource.

A Note on Editing and Performance Practice

Most Baroque and early Classical composers wrote few dynamics, articulation, or other performance indications in their scores. Interpretation was left up to the performer, with the expectation that the performance practice was understood. In this edition, therefore, most of the dynamics and tempo indications in the Baroque and early Classical pieces have been added by the editors. These editorial markings, including fingering and the execution of ornaments, are intended to be helpful rather than definitive.

The keyboard instruments of the 17th and early 18th centuries lacked the sustaining power of the modern piano. Consequently, the usual keyboard touch was detached rather than legato. The pianist should assume that a lightly detached touch is appropriate for Baroque and early Classical music, unless a different approach is indicated by the style of the music.

Even into the 19th century, composers' scores could vary from copy to copy or edition to edition. Thus, the editors of the *Celebration Series®* have also made editorial choices in much of the Classical and Romantic repertoire presented in the series.

This edition follows the policy that the bar line cancels accidentals. In accordance with current practice, cautionary accidentals are added only in cases of possible ambiguity.

Teachers and students should refer to the companion guides – the *Student Workbooks* and the *Handbook for Teachers* – for further discussion of style and pedagogical elements. For examination requirements of The Royal Conservatory of Music, please refer to the current *Piano Syllabus*.

Dr. Trish Sauerbrei
Editor-in-Chief

Contents

Prelude and Fugue in D Major
BWV 850

Johann Sebastian Bach
(1685 – 1750)

Praeludium ♩ = 126 – 138

For examinations, the *Prelude* and the Fugue are to be played as one selection.

Source: *Das Wohltemperierte Clavier*, book 1 (1722)

6

For examinations, the *Prelude* and the *Fugue* are to be played as one selection.

0-88797-703-0 / 06

French Suite No. 5

BWV 816

Allemande

Johann Sebastian Bach
(1685 – 1750)

For examinations, *Allemande* and *Gigue* are to be played as one selection.
Source: *French Suites,* BWV 812-817 (1722 – 1725)

Gigue

For examinations, *Allemande* and *Gigue* are to be played as one selection.

12

Capriccio sopra la lontananza del fratello dilettissimo

Capriccio on the absence of a most beloved brother

BWV 992

IV

Johann Sebastian Bach
(1685 – 1750)

Allhier kommen die Freunde (weil sie doch sehen, daß es anders nicht sein kann) und nehmen Abschied. *

* Seeing that it cannot be otherwise, his friends gather together to bid him farewell.

The chords in mm. 1 – 3 can be rolled.
For examinations, movements IV, V, and VI are to be played as one selection.

This six-movement programmatic work, composed *ca* 1703 – 1706, is thought to commemorate the departure of
J.S. Bach's elder brother, Johann Jakob Bach (1682 – 1722), for Sweden, where he had accepted a position as
oboist in the service of King Charles XII. Each movement bears a descriptive title.

V: Aria di Postiglione

For examinations, movements IV, V, and VI are to be played as one selection.

VI: Fuga all' imitatione di Posta

For examinations, movements IV, V, and VI are to be played as one selection.

18

Sonata in E Major
op. 14, no. 1

I

Ludwig van Beethoven
(1770 – 1827)

Composed 1798
For examinations, either the first and second movements *or* the second and third movements are to be
played as one selection.

20

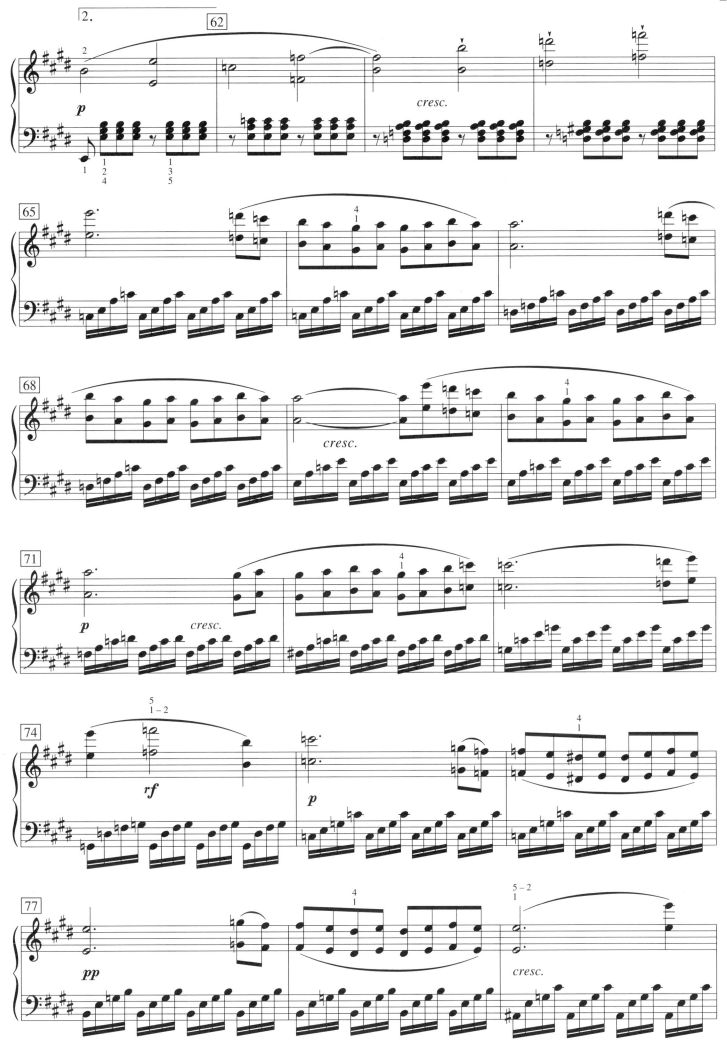

22

24

II

For examinations, either the first and second movements *or* the second and third movements are to be played as one selection.

26

III: Rondo

For examinations, either the first and second movements *or* the second and third movements are to be played as one selection.

28

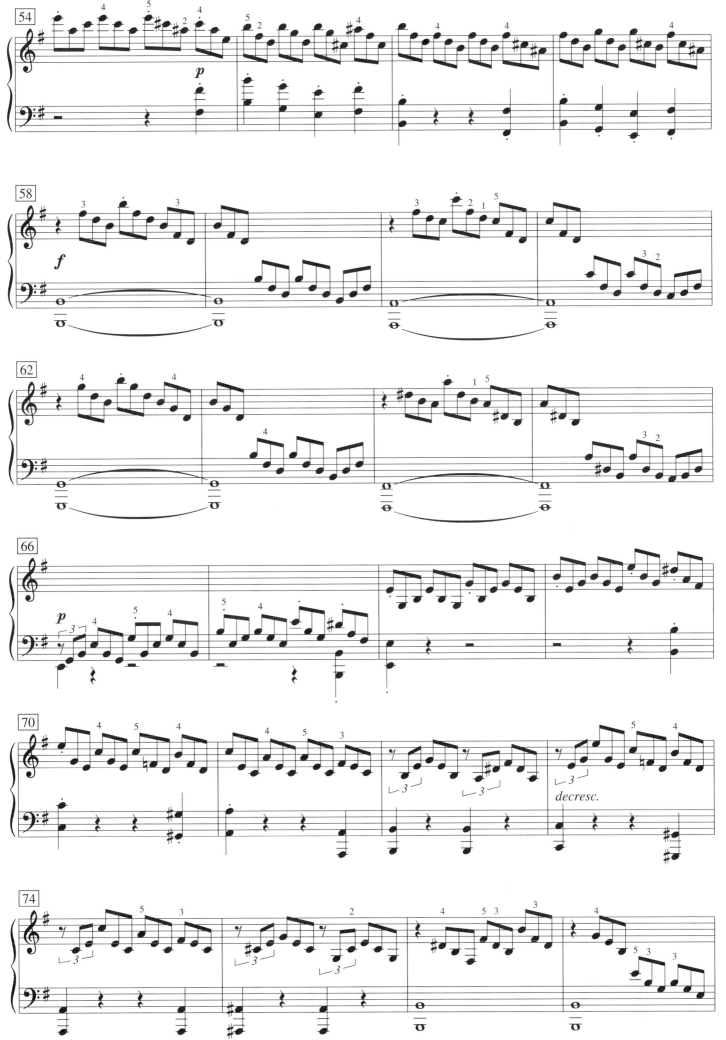

30

Sonata in B Minor
Hob. XVI:32
I

Franz Joseph Haydn
(1732 – 1809)

For examinations, the complete sonata is to be played as one selection.

Haydn composed 6 sonatas, Hob. XVI:27 – 32, in 1774 – 1776.

II

Menuet ♩ = 76 – 84

For examinations, the complete sonata is to be played as one selection.

III: Finale

For examinations, the complete sonata is to be played as one selection.

42

Sonata in E flat Major
K 282 (189g)

I

Wolfgang Amadeus Mozart
(1756 – 1791)

Composed 1774
For examinations, the complete sonata is to be played as one selection.

44

(d) Play as short *appoggiatura*.

Coda

46

II

For examinations, the complete sonata is to be played as one selection.

48

III

Allegro ♩ = 116 – 120

For examinations, the complete sonata is to be played as one selection.

Waltz in E Minor
op. posth.

Fréderic Chopin
(1810 – 1849)

Composed 1830

52

53

54

Nocturne in F sharp Major
op. 15, no. 2

Fréderic Chopin
(1810 – 1849)

Doppio movimento

58

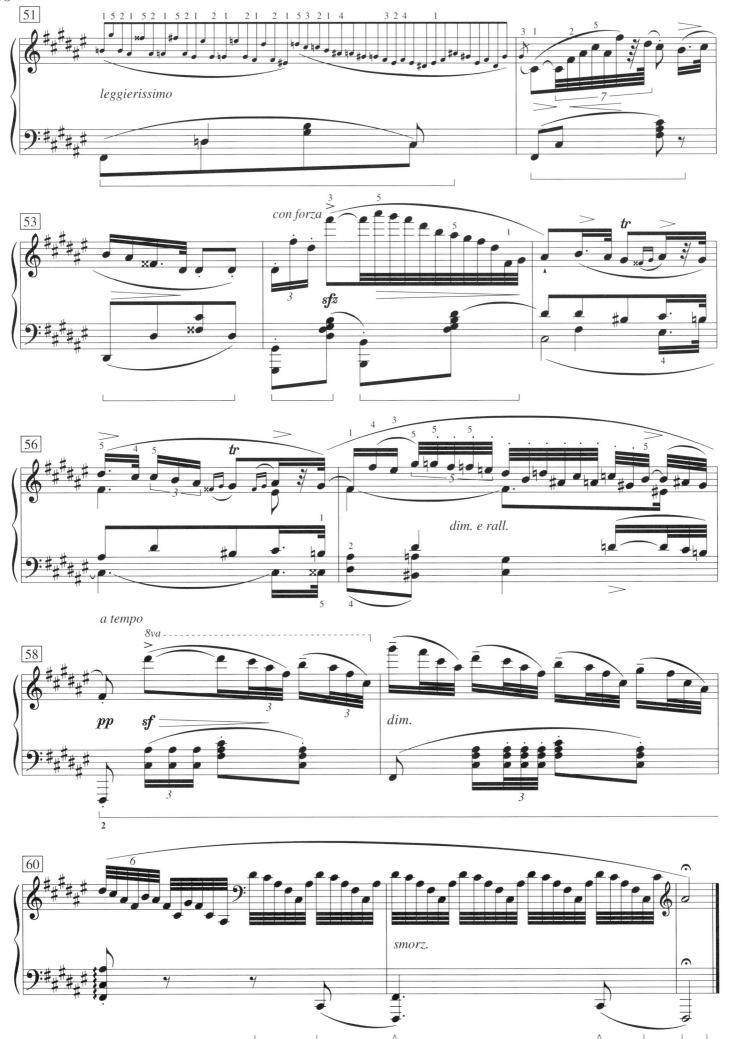

Ballade in D Minor

op. 10, no. 1

Nach der Schottischen Ballade "Edward" in Herder's *Stimmen der Völker**

Johannes Brahms
(1833 – 1897)

Composed 1854
* After the Scottish Ballade "Edward" in Herder's *Stimmen der Völker*
Source: *Vier Balladen*, op. 10

60

Impromptu in E flat Major

op. 90, no. 2

Franz Schubert
(1797 – 1828)

Source: *Vier Impromptus für Klavier*, op. 90, D 899 (1827)

64

66

68

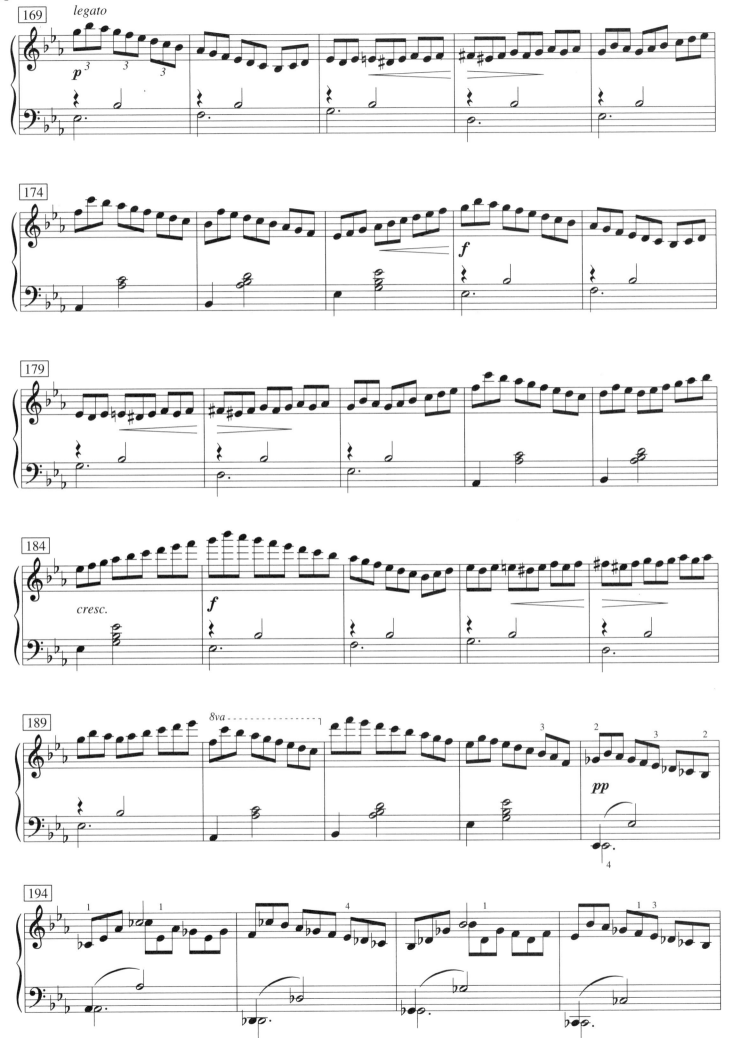

Coda

Intermezzo
op. 26, no. 4

Robert Schumann
(1810 – 1856)

Mit größter Energie * ♩ = 100 – 112

* With great energy

Source: *Faschingsschwank aus Wien*, op. 26 (1839)

74

Mélodie

Melody

op. 3, no. 3

Sergei Rachmaninoff
(1873 – 1943)

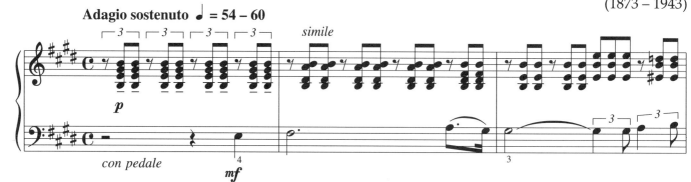

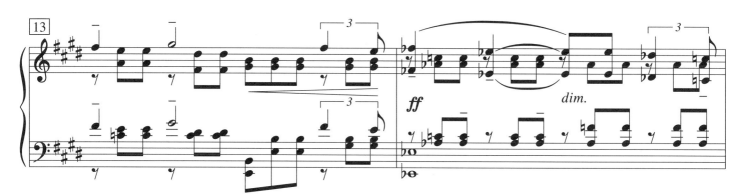

Source: *Morceaux de fantaisie,* op. 3 (1892)

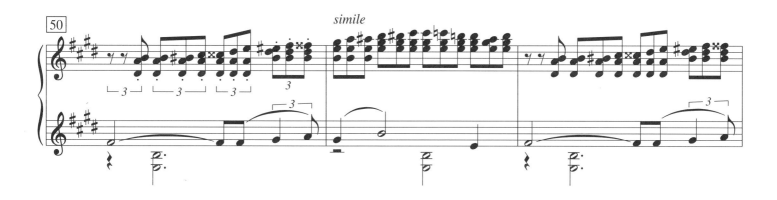

Lotus Land
op. 47, no. 1

Cyril Scott
(1879 – 1970)

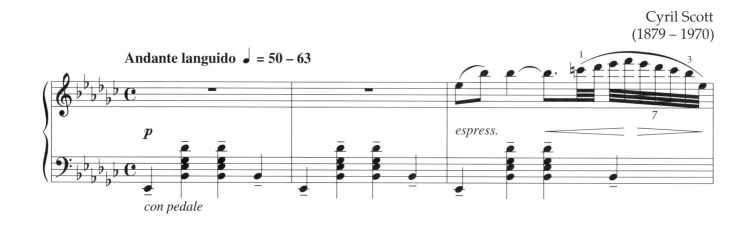

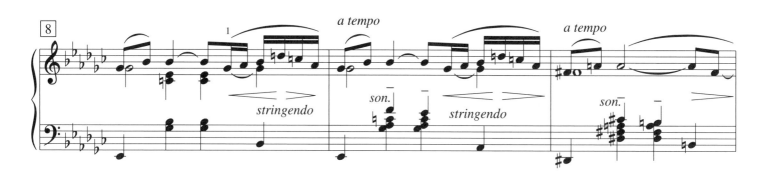

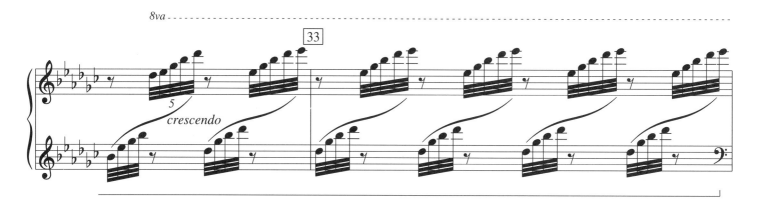

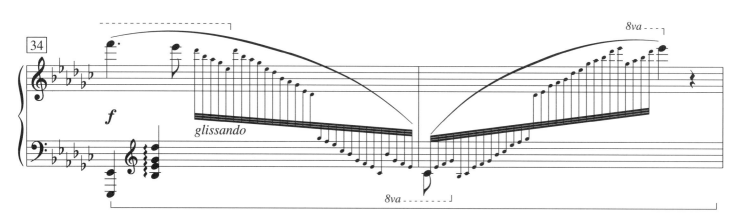

84

Brouillards
Mist

Claude Debussy
(1862 – 1918)

Modéré ♪ = 84 – 88
extrêmement égal et léger
la m.g. un peu en valeur sur la m.d. *

* Extremely even and light; emphasize the left hand a little more than the right.
Source: *Préludes*, 2ᵉ livre (1912 – 1913)

0-88797-703-0 / 85

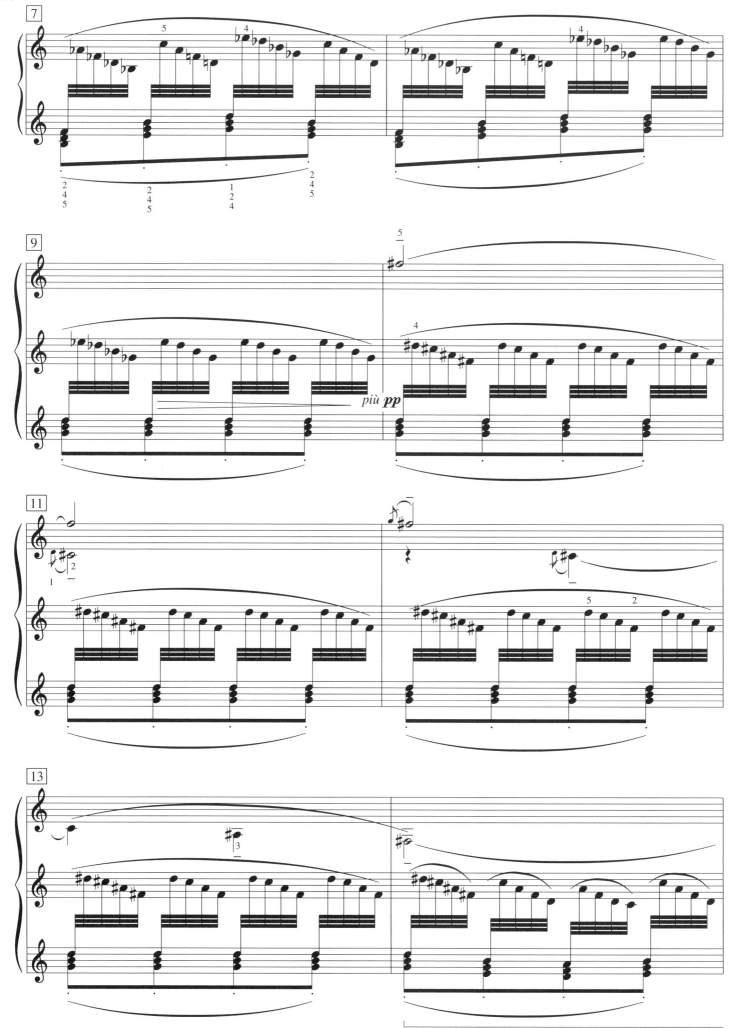

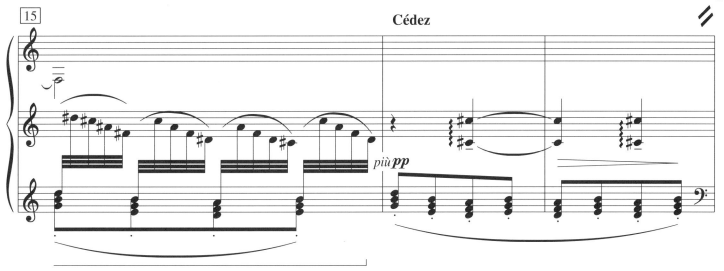

Cédez

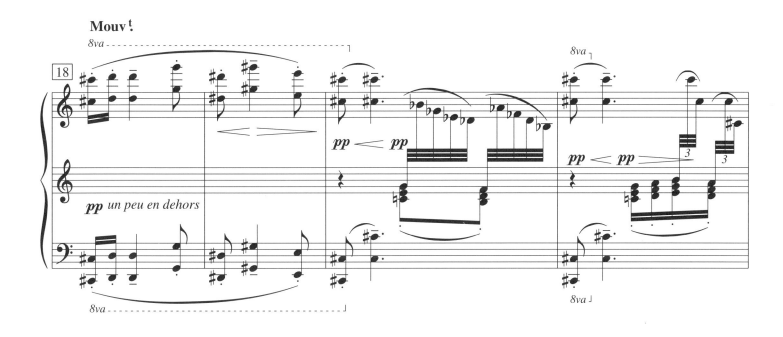

Mouv.ᵗ

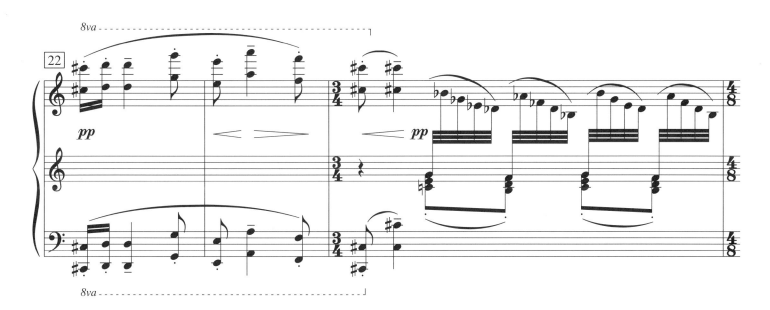

88

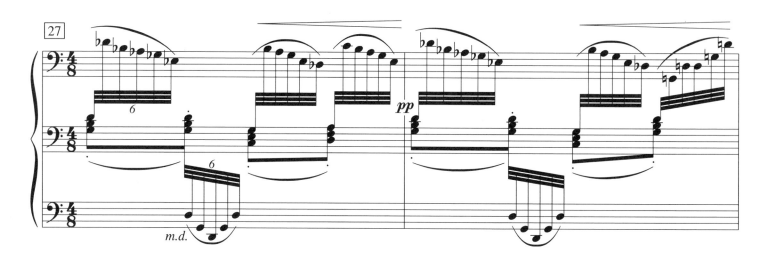

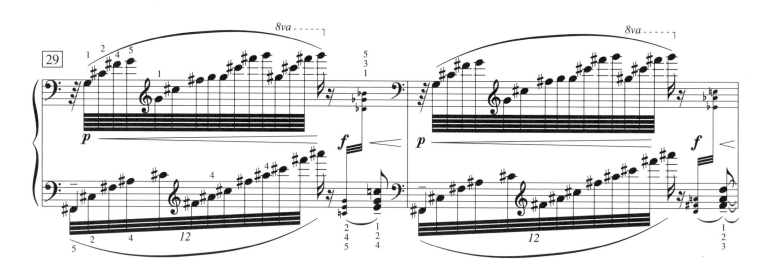

Un peu retenu

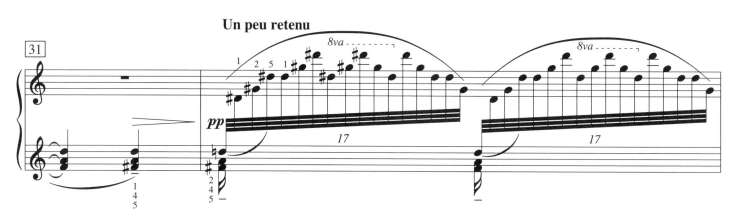

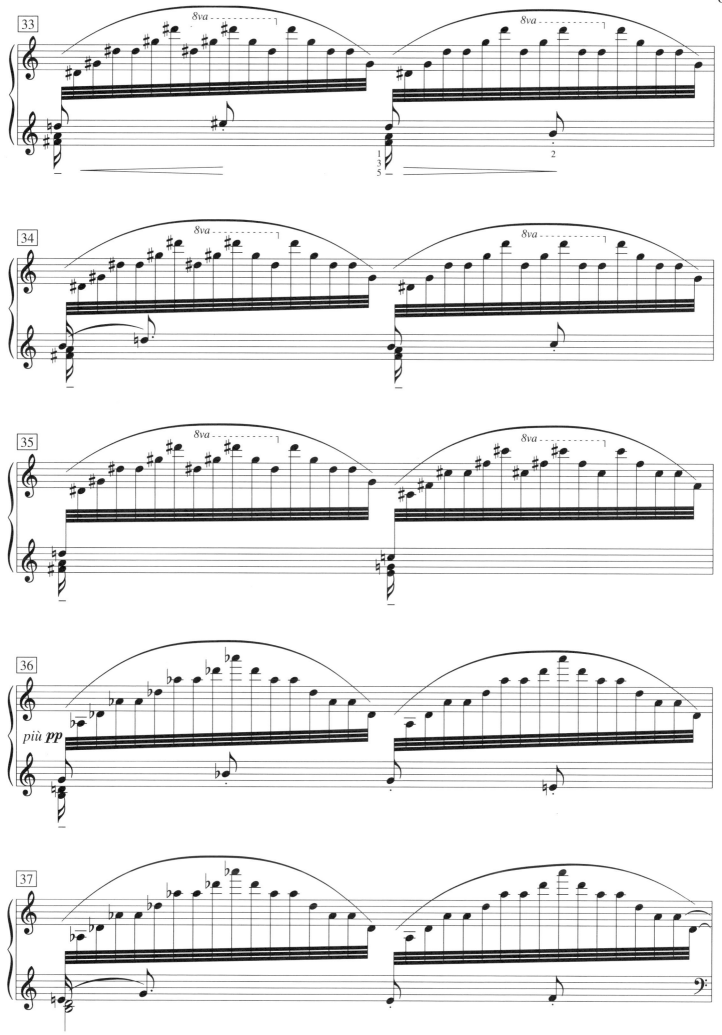

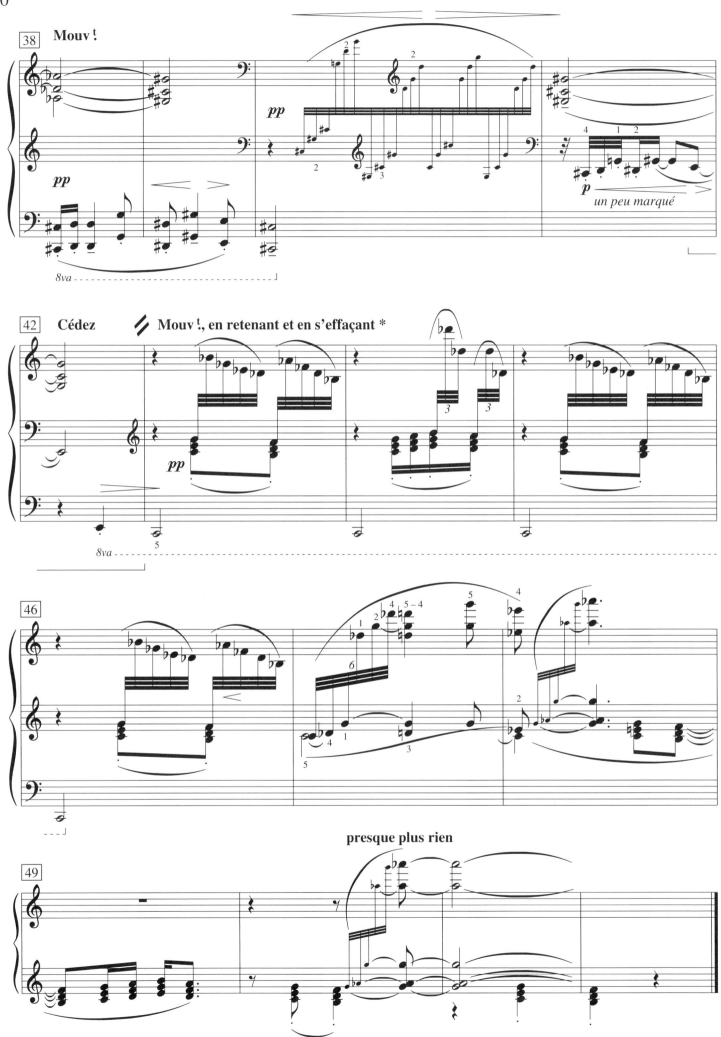

* a tempo, then slowly fading away

Suite française

III. Petite marche militaire

Francis Poulenc
(1899 – 1963)

Mouvement de pas redoublé ♩ = 104 – 120

For examinations, movements III, VI, and VII are to be played as one selection.

Source: *Suite française, d'après Claude Gervaise* (chamber version 1935, piano version 1936)

© Copyright 1935 Editions Durand, Paris, France. Reprinted by permission of the publisher.

92

VI: Sicilienne

For examinations, movements III, VI, and VII are to be played as one selection.

0-88797-703-0 / 93

VII: Carillon

For examinations, movements III, VI, and VII are to be played as one selection.

96

Danse du meunier
The Miller's Dance

Manuel de Falla
(1876 – 1946)

Source: *farruca* (Spanish flamenco dance) from *El sombrero de tres picos* (1919)

100

* Use the *una corda* pedal as well as the damper pedal.

A Hermit Thrush at Eve

op. 92, no. 1

Holy, Holy! — in the hush
Hearken to the hermit thrush
All the air is in prayer

John Vance Cheney

Amy Marcy Cheney Beach
(1867 – 1944)

The small notes in this composition, e.g., mm. 23–27, are exact notations, an octave lower, of bird calls heard by the composer at the MacDowell Colony in Peterborough, New Hampshire. The song of the hermit thrush alternates between held notes and rapid notes which outline triads and chords of the seventh.

Composed 1921

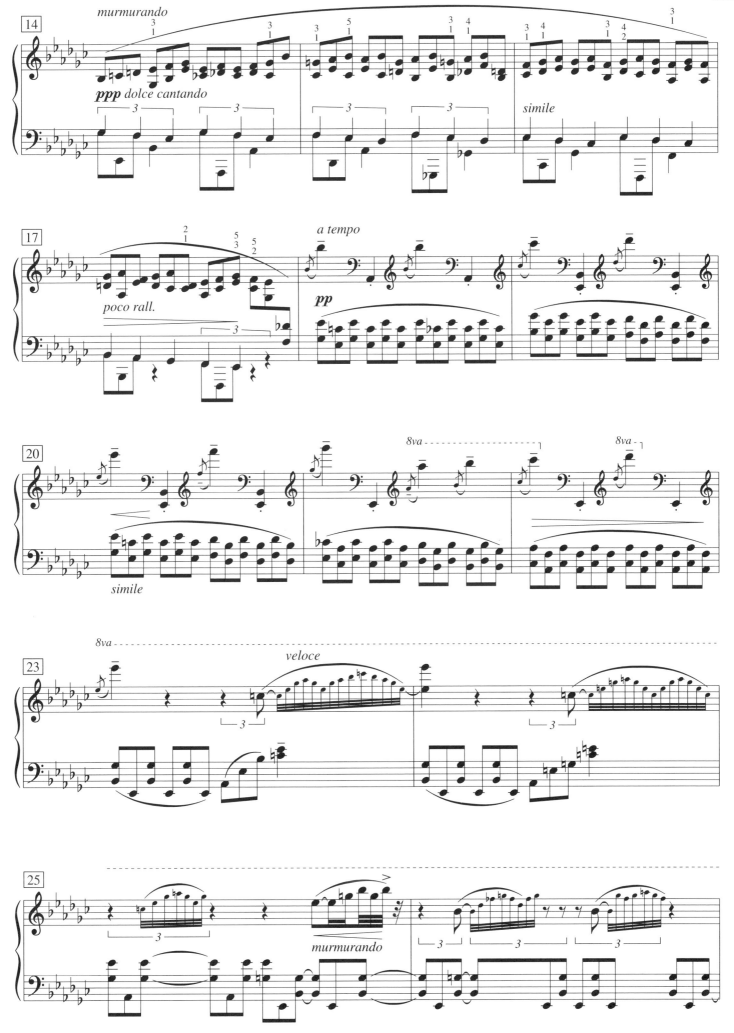

106

Rondo No. 1
op. 84

Béla Bartók
(1881 – 1945)

Composed 1916

Source: *Három rondo népi dallamokkal* [Three rondos on Slovak folk tunes], op. 84

© Copyright 1930 Universal Edition. Copyright renewed 1957 Boosey & Hawkes, New York. Reprinted by permission of Boosey & Hawkes, Inc.

108

110

The Cat and the Mouse

Scherzo humoristique

Aaron Copland
(1920 – 1990)

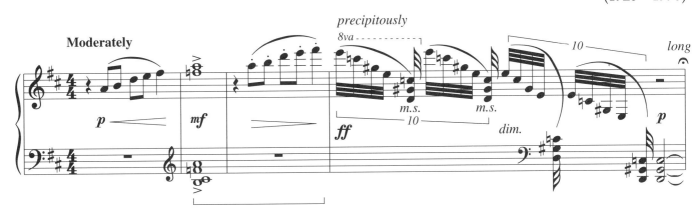

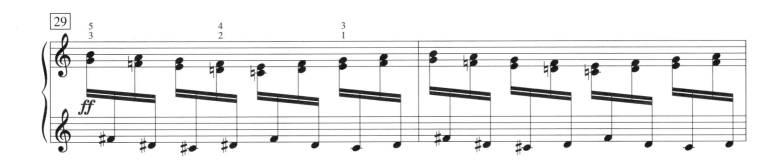

Very much slower

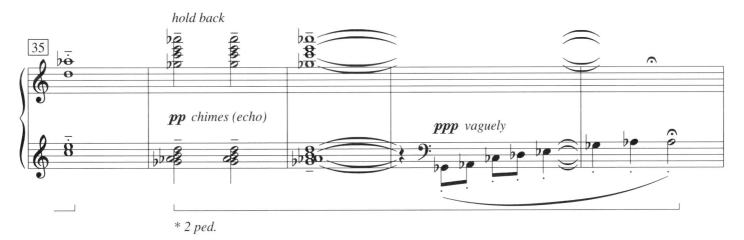

hold back

pp chimes (echo)

ppp vaguely

* 2 ped.

* Depress the damper pedal and the *una corda* pedal simultaneously.

0-88797-703-0 / 113

114

116

Trois pièces pour la légende dorée

Three Pieces for the Golden Legend

I: Prélude

Clermont Pépin
(1926 –   )

The use of the pedal is left to the performer's discretion.
For examinations, all three pieces are to be played as one selection.

119

II: Interlude

The use of the pedal is left to the performer's discretion.
For examinations, all three pieces are to be played as one selection.

III: Toccate

For examinations, all three pieces are to be played as one selection.

Plainte calme
Gentle Sorrow

Olivier Messiaen
(1908 – 1992)

* Bring out the melody and the inner voice.

Source: *Huit préludes pour piano* (1929)

Three Fantastic Dances
op. 5
I

Dmitri Shostakovich
(1906 – 1975)

For examinations, all three dances are to be played as one selection.
Composed 1920 – 1922

Permission to reprint granted by G. Schirmer, Inc. (ASCAP); Boosey & Hawkes, Inc.; International Musikverlage Hans Sikorski;
Casa Ricordi-BMG Ricordi; Le Chant du Monde; and Zenon Music Company Ltd. for their respective territories. 0-88797-703-0 / 126

II

For examinations, all three dances are to be played as one selection.

III

For examinations, all three dances are to be played as one selection.

Rondó sobre temas infantiles argentinos
Rondo on Argentine Children's Folk-tunes

Alberto Ginastera
(1916 – 1983)

to Reginald Godden

Strangeness of Heart

Harry Somers
(1925 – 1999)

Composed 1942

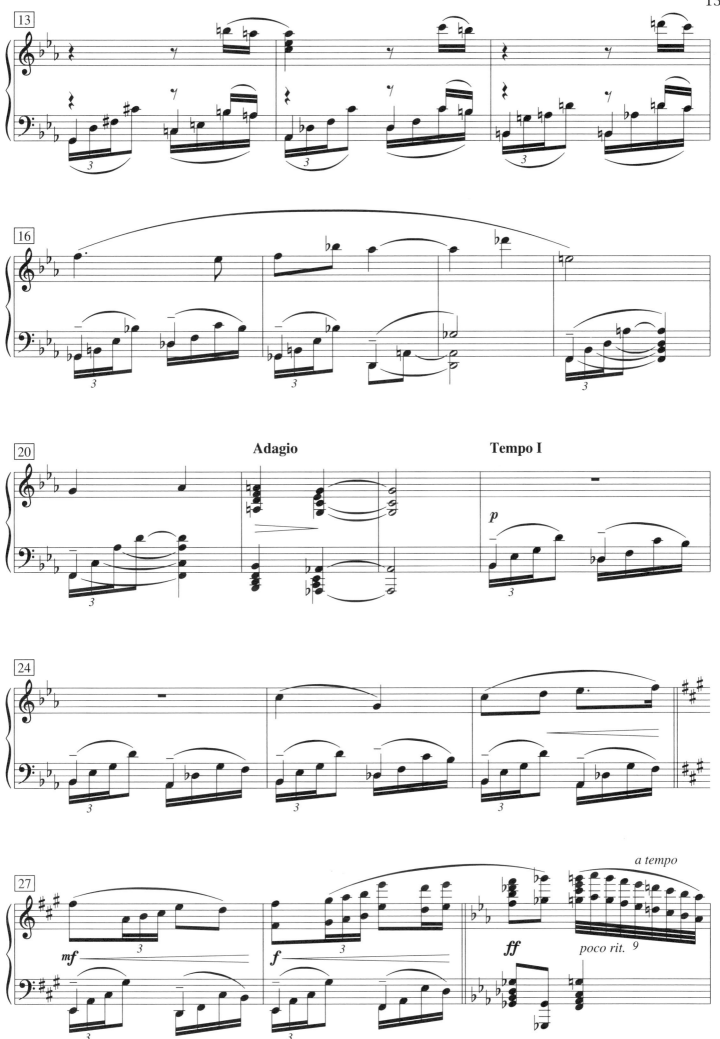

Pas de deux

Samuel Barber
(1910 – 1981)

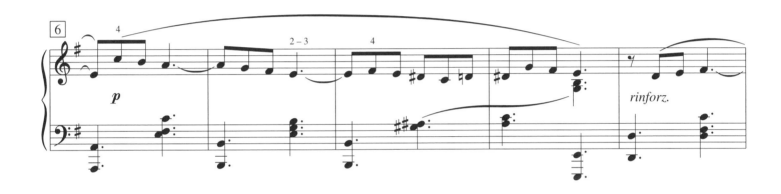

Source: *Souvenirs*, op. 28 (1952)

Prelude
op. 7, no. 1

Lee Hoiby
(1926 –   )

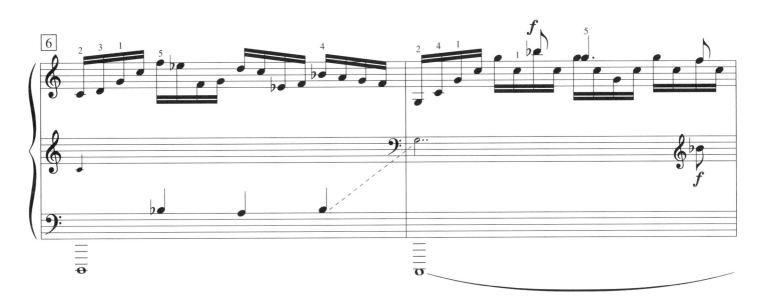

* The small notes indicate parts of the melody that are duplicated in another voice.

Source: *Five Preludes,* op. 7 (revised)

Variations in A Minor
op. 40, no. 2

Dmitri Kabalevsky
(1904 – 1987)

Source: *Variations for Piano*, op. 40
Permission to reprint granted by G. Schirmer, Inc. (ASCAP); Boosey & Hawkes, Inc.; Internationale Musikverlage Hans Sikorski; Le Chant du Monde; and Zenon Music Company Ltd. for their respective territories.

Variation II
Più mosso

Variation IV
Poco più mosso

Variation V
Allegro molto

Six Preludes, op. 6

Prelude No. 1

Robert Muczynski
(1929 –   )

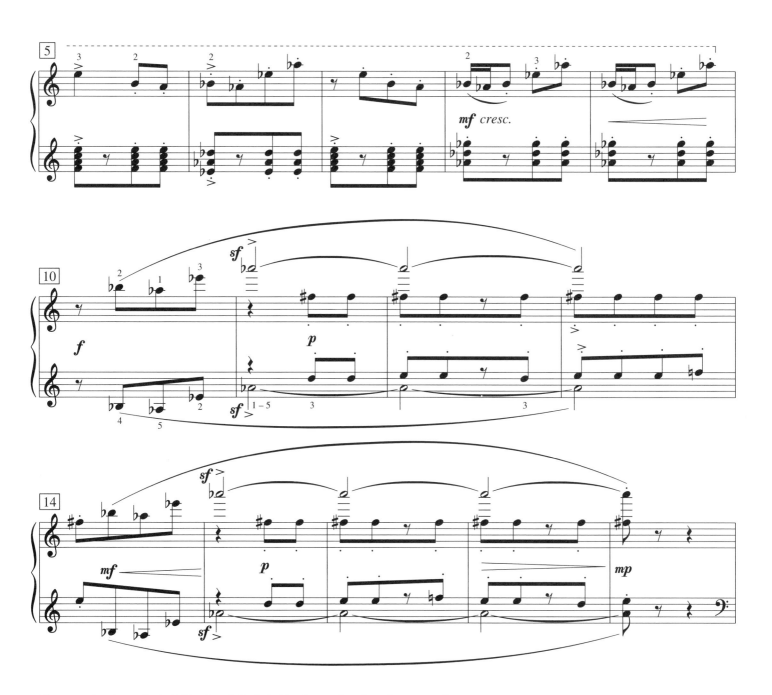

For examinations, *Prelude No. 1* and *Prelude No. 6* must be played as one selection.

Source: *Six Preludes,* op. 6

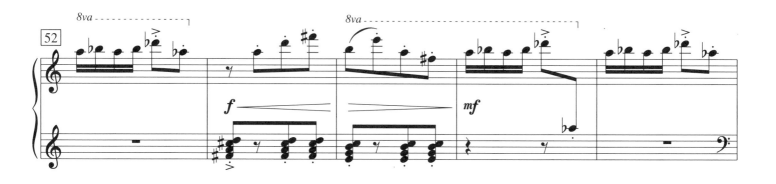

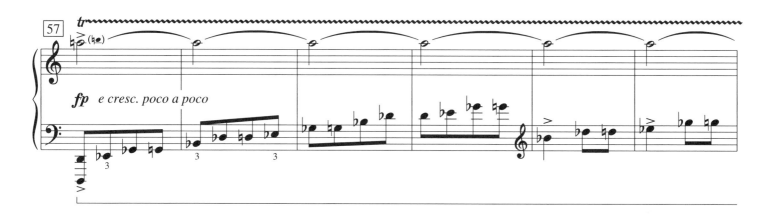

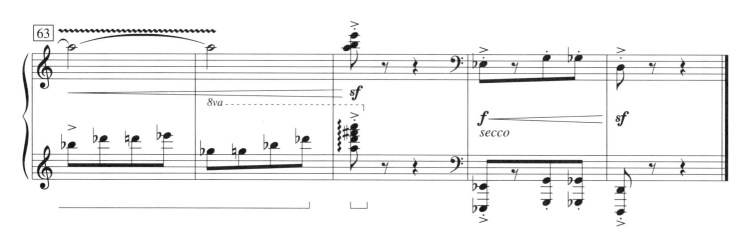

Prelude No. 6

For examinations, *Prelude No. 1* and *Prelude No. 6* must be played as one selection.

158

Four Bagatelles

Bagatelle No. 2

Ann Southam
(1937 –)

For examinations, *Bagatelle No. 2* and *Bagatelle No. 4* must be played as one selection.

Source: *Four Bagatelles* (1971)

Bagatelle No. 4

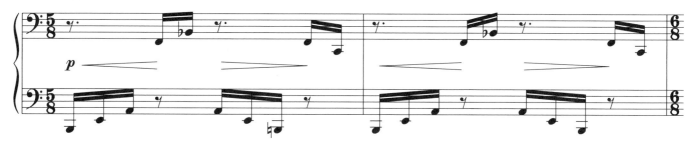

For examinations, *Bagatelle No. 2* and *Bagatelle No. 4* must be played as one selection.

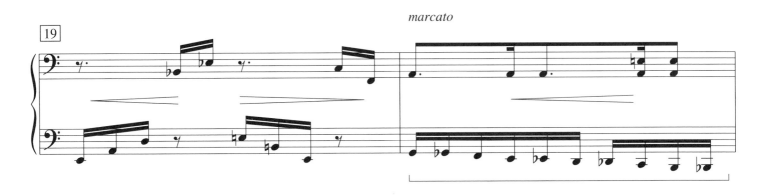

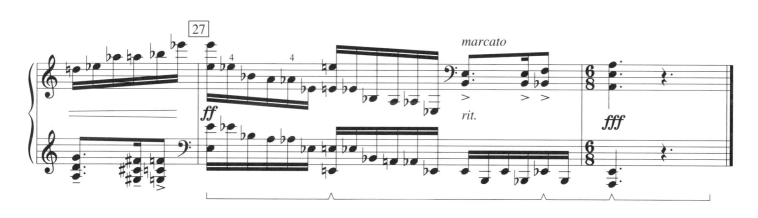

Snow Games

Christos Tsitsaros
(1961 –   )

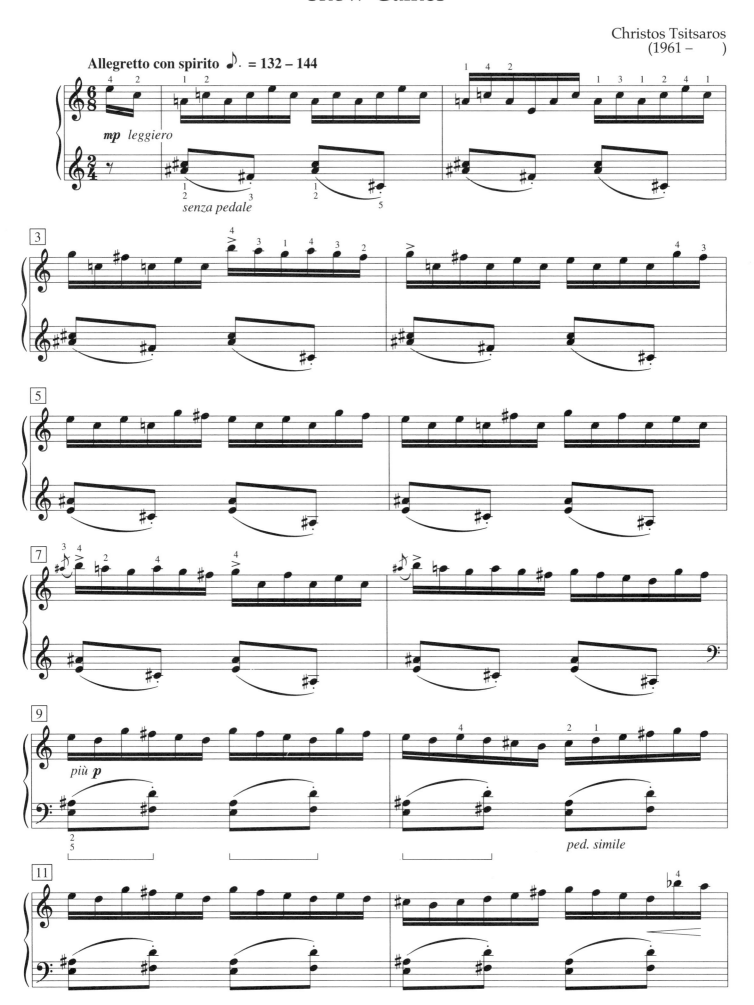

Source: *Nine Tales*
© Copyright 1996 The Frederick Harris Music Co., Limited, Mississauga, Ontario, Canada.

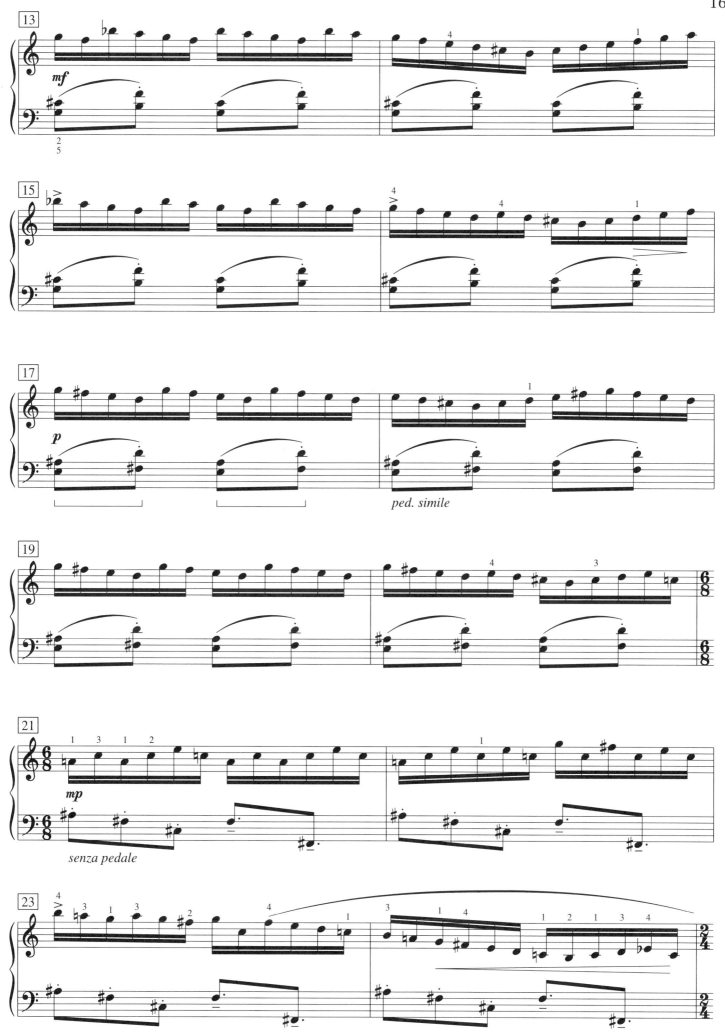